Anonymous

A Hint Upon the Present Debates on Indian Affairs

Anonymous

A Hint Upon the Present Debates on Indian Affairs

ISBN/EAN: 9783337059200

Printed in Europe, USA, Canada, Australia, Japan

Cover: Foto ©Suzi / pixelio.de

More available books at **www.hansebooks.com**

A HINT

UPON THE PRESENT

DEBATES

ON

INDIAN AFFAIRS.

Fiat Justitia, ruat Cælum.

LONDON:

Printed for J. FIELDING, in Pater-Noster-Row.
MDCCLXXXII.
[Price One Shilling.]

A

HINT, &c.

AN idea has for some little time prevailed, that the two Committees for examining Indian affairs (however originally disconnected in their powers, and the nature or destination of their appointments) were inclined to coalesce: particularly in their votes of personal censure. — To those who considered the different subjects on which their proceedings commenced; who could not comprehend wherein the invasion of Hyder Ally in the Carnatic, or the struggles of the Mahrattas in Guzerat, could be affected by the administration of civil and criminal justice in Bengal, such a conjunction did not at first seem likely: experience has at length proved it to exist; at least the coincidence of the resolutions lately exhibited by the several Chairmen of the Committees, strongly countenances this belief.——The steady love of justice, the sincere regard to candour and impartiality, which actuate each of those very respectable bodies, are not to be called in question. It is to such venerable qualities, joined with the acutest discernment, and the most extensive talents, to which the writer of this, and every honest man, must exultingly make his appeal. The strength of reasoning, and the splendor of eloquence, which have

already

already been so amply and so ably employed on Indian subjects by all the first abilities of this or any age, almost preclude the possibility of contributing a new thought or an elegant phrase to the present discussion. —But the Reports (those honourable testimonies of the labour, the candour, the dignity, which have assisted in their compilation) are still free for examination. Upon the facts there recorded, each man is at liberty to form his own judgment, and to compare, according to the portion of understanding he may possess, the scope of the resolutions now pending, with the tenor of the Reports from whence they are drawn. Different men will of course found their opinion on different facts, or different opinions on the same fact: the result of the public decision will undoubtedly be more strictly just, as the aggregate body of opinions covers the greater space of ground: and while a topic of such magnitude is still open to consideration, no hint, however trifling, but may have some weight; no spark however small, but may conduce by some lucky accident to kindle a flame that may light to the most important discoveries.

The late resolutions founded on part of the fifth and the whole of the sixth Report of the Committee of secrecy, tend principally to affix an idea of political injustice and unwarrantable thirst for conquest on the court of directors of the East-India Company, and on the Governor General and supreme council of Bengal.— The body indeed of the sixth Report, after the most careful and repeated perusals, does not offer an insinuation of the kind: and therefore it can only be sought in the appendix, which, unfortunately for our hopes of fuller information, is still unpublished.

We can only therefore suppose, that from the contents of that appendix may be deduced incontrovertible proofs of the propriety and necessity of each Resolution — and we must in the mean time rest satisfied

fied with the bare assertion " that the protection and
" assistance afforded to Ragoba, and a wish to add to
" the advantages *said* to have been procured by the
" treaty of Poorunder, were the sole and absolute cause
" as well as object of the Mahratta war."—The report itself merely shews " that the Governor general
of Bengal agreed with the sentiments of his employers the Directors and those of the council of Bombay, in reprobating the terms of that treaty," " that
the articles of it had not been punctually fulfilled by
the parties;" and " that new cause of uneasiness
had arisen from the open favour afforded by the
Poonah Durbar to an agent of France." With these
events the report opens—and the subsequent pages
are almost wholly occupied by a studied display of
that opposition, which the measures of the Governor
general for the alternative of " *honourable peace* or
vigorous war" on the western side of India, met with
in every stage from the two junior members of his
council.

It is here necessary to observe, that this boasted
treaty of Poorunder was an early measure of general
Clavering's majority; that it was set on foot contrary to the opinion and vote of the two most experienced members of the supreme council (indeed
of those two who alone had any experience at all);
that it was generally thought to have been purchased
by the sacrifice of the company's nearest and dearest
interests; that on those principles it was loudly protested against by the council of Bombay, with the
decisive superiority of local knowledge; and that it
was received with disapprobation by the court of directors, in whom lay (or was thought to lie) the
power of deciding on the general merits and actions
of all their servants: proofs of all which assertions
abound in every page of the 5th and 6th reports.—
Moreover, the 16th resolution expresly affirms,
" that the directors, by their letters of 5th February
" and 16th April, 1777 manifested some dissatisfaction
" at

"at the terms of the treaty of Poorunder, and as it had not procured for the company the surrender of Bassein," gave great encouragements to all their servants to use their utmost endeavours for more favourable conditions.—Now, if from these premises it be admitted that the court of directors stimulated their servants abroad to those actions which the wisdom of the Committee has thought good to censure as deficient in moderation, policy, and good faith; if *their* instructions be allowed to have been the motive of the Governor general's conduct; He, in acting up to the declared sentiments of his immediate employers, to whom in the great line of duty he was bound to submit, undoubtedly cannot with justice be an object of the same censure. He has proved faithful to the express commands of his employers—he has therefore given proofs of his worthiness to be employed again.

But tho' the 6th report, as has been already observed, cannot by any implication be brought to bear a criminatory shape, the resolutions founded on it convey a decided condemnation on all the capital measures which have marked Mr. Hastings's government. For the grounds of that condemnation we are therefore of course referred to the appendix yet unborn—and if we were now in possession of it, no arguments can thence be deduced, but such as have already dropped from the prompt pens of the opposing members of the superior council—these may *perhaps* be numerous and solid—(that they are worked up with all the artifice of party zeal, and all the tinsel of interested eloquence, is well known) but all the powers of truth and of candour must cry out that they *are* not, *cannot* be satisfactory or conclusive—Mr. Hastings has repeatedly answered them—irresistably refuted them all—such at least as were founded in any thing but malice or personality. Surely it would not have been unworthy of the trouble, or beneath the dignity of the Committee to have

urged

urged some reasons from itself, some new and impartial reasons, for the introduction of such a severe series of censure. If every political negotiation, every stroke in the cabinet or the field during Mr. Hastings's actual enjoyment of authority, must be racked at the tribunal of rebuke, the instruments already applied by general Clavering's party to that service, are too effectually blunted to do much execution.

The political contest as it stood at Bengal, must surely, by the most cursory reader of the disgusting volumes which contain it, be deemed at least to have ended in a drawn battle—if he will not allow the victory, as it clearly stands, to be with the Governor general. To join issue then with the Committee on the grounds of their own appendix—while it contains no plea for the censure of Mr. Hastings, but such as is gathered from the violent and clamorous minutes of Mr. Francis and his assistants, the public will draw from the same source ample proofs of the Governor general's *wisdom, policy, moderation, good-faith,* and above all of his steady adherence to the real interests of his employers. He will there be found to plead his own defence with such a cogency of argument, such an adherence to fact, and such a display of superior information, as must inevitably insure to him, in the opinion of the world, that full acquittal, and that merited applause, which he has at length so victoriously obtained from his long-deluded masters.

An indifferent auditor of the debates on India matters, would naturally recollect, that, by the original *Regulating Act*, the Directors of the East India Company were enjoined to communicate to his Majesty's secretaries of state all the information they should receive respecting the politics of India, and all the orders they meant to issue in consequence. He would then ask, whether or not this duty had been regularly performed—whether any proof existed of failure in the mode

mode of compliance to this regulation, or of unwillingness to abide by such alterations in the orders intended to be issued, as the ministry might think fit to recommend. Having been satisfied in these points, he would conceive that the Directors must at once stand exonerated from any retrospective recrimination on the subject of all such orders, admitted (and so tacitly approved) by his Majesty's Ministers. For otherwise, what could be the intention of parliament in framing this regulation? And if the Directors be thus virtually armed with the shield of a higher authority, there is infinitely greater cause to admit, that their own immediate servants acting under the decided approbation of their masters, and under the implied consent of the executive powers of the state, must be clearly and *ipso facto* acquitted. All political responsibility must be confined, as it should seem, to two heads, the construction of indecisive orders — or attention to state necessity: and in both cases the success of the measure adopted is the usual criterion for the merits of the Statesman, and still more for those of the company's servant. The Directors, as a commercial body, governed by the general rules of mercantile transactions, and setting the gains against the risks of all adventures, have been in use to consider territorial acquisitions in India as lucky strokes in trade, the profits whereof were regularly and without scruple carried to account. (No impeachment on their honesty and good faith, notwithstanding.) They found the *jus fortioris* to be universally allowed in Asia: and, perhaps, like able merchants, adopted (as they had good reason), in their several dealings with Indians, *the custom of the Indian market.* This may be thought irony—but it is common sense. A short revisal of the Company's affairs through the rise and progress of its Asiatic power, and a little attention to the influence of those circumstances which have uniformly biassed the conduct of every European nation in its connexion with India, will presently decide the fact.

The

The principles of commerce were by no means accurately underſtood when the Portugueſe firſt ſailed to India. It is not then extraordinary, that rather than return to Europe without cargoes, they ſhould force a trade where they could not perſuade it. Being conſidered as interlopers, they were obliged to aſſume a ſuitable conduct in their own defence, and to aſſert the preference of the market by the rhetoric of the muſket. Every where ſurrounded with hollow friends, jarring rivals, and inſidious competitors, they had no refuge but in their own force—where they could not impoſe quiet, they were ſure of moleſtation. Hence the advance from an *occaſional* reſidence to a *fixed* factory, from an open dwelling to a tenable fort, from a dependance on the capricious protection of a barbarous prince, to a vigorous reliance on their own ſtrength, was in ſome caſes ſilent and gradual—but in moſt rapid and inſtantaneous. By the ſteady and well-applied exertions of their own military ſuperiority, they ſoon acquired a deciſive influence over all India, and ſecured that influence by extenſive territories. War was now grown to a ſyſtem, and plunder to a regular courſe of trade. They ſcoured the Seacoaſts from Point Natal to Cape Comorin, and from thence to the extremities of China. They had every where armies on the continent and on the iſlands: and they maintained at different times war with all the different powers of the peninſula, and occaſionally with ſeveral at once. But war never ruined the Portugueſe.—The change of meaſures which conſtantly attended the change of governors—that fatal policy which invented a *triennial* adminiſtration—unhinged all the main ſprings of government, and reduced the holders of public offices to the neceſſity of " ſeeking what they might devour" (from the public or wherever it was to be found), " knowing they had " but a ſhort time."———The languor, the corruption, the diſunion attendant on ſo ruinous a ſyſtem, did not eſcape the eager penetration of ſelf-intereſt in their

B *com-*

commercial rivals the Dutch, who alſo made political alliances, acquired territory, and maintained armies, *all in the way of trade.* Yet *they* at leaſt (whatever may be ſaid of the Portugueſe) were in the beginning of the laſt century the patterns of frugality, of prudence, and of mercantile regularity, to all Europe; and indeed ſo they continue to this day.——For, tho' they have never relinquiſhed one foot of ground in Aſia which they could by any means appropriate: tho' by a ſtretch of management unknown in the annals of the world, they ſecured to themſelves a monopoly of ſpice by ſeizing all the widely-diſtant places which produced it,—they ſtill perſevere in the ſimple and uniform plan of conduct to which they owed their firſt ſucceſs.—The ſame mode of adminiſtration, which was originally preſcribed to their firſt infant factory, has proved of ſo pliant and univerſal a nature, as to ſuit every different ſize and deſcription of government to which they have progreſſively ſucceeded.—And it is this undeviating attention to conſiſtency of meaſures which alone has guaranteed their political exiſtence thro' every poſſible combination and revolution of things in the four quarters of the world.

The inſatiable ſearch of modern curioſity has in ſome degree developped the advantage of their ſyſtem. But the Dutch have ever been wiſer—no unproſperous turn of their affairs (and that they have not been privileged from the general inſtability of ſublunary events, witneſs the loſs of that very valuable iſland Formoſa) ever tempted them to an indiſcreet diſplay of their wealth and their reſources—they have continued to ſell their ſpice, and to be ſilent. Nor has the national government at home, by any intemperate interference with the affairs of their company, ever drawn forth from the ſhelves of the compting-houſe thoſe important records on which depended the proſperity, and perhaps the very being of ſo grand a member of the ſtate: ſo that the profits of their territories in point of revenue, and the means by which they are

rendered

rendered productive, still remain an impenetrable political arcanum.——

Britain has been the last of the commercial nations of Europe to avail herself decidedly of her arms in promotion of her mercantile concerns. Territory has every where been forced on her by the necessity of resisting unprovoked attacks, and of conquering in her own defence. The incursions of the Mahrattas into Bengal, under Ally Verdy Khan's subahship, had furnished the Dutch with a plausible pretence for fortifying their settlement of Chinsura. The old fort at Calcutta arose at the same time, and for the same purpose of protecting our peaceable factors; tho' it could oppose no effectual resistance to the unmerited assaults of an avaricious tyrant. But fortune soon declared in our favour: the aggressor was repulsed in his turn; and a course of victory, well followed up, gave us the unexpected possession of a mighty territory. Other events, equally unforeseen, have led us to a participation of the powers of government in the Carnatic.——Here let us indulge a moment's reflection.——Had the same ideas of *moderation*, and principles of mere *self-defence*, then gone forth, which have lately grown so much into vogue,—had prohibitory condemnations of all schemes or enlargement of dominion been *then* issued,—it will be worth while to turn back a few pages of oriental history, and compare our probable situation on that supposition, to our actual one under a more accommodating set of regulations. We will, for instance, conceive Lord Clive, at the two grand periods of his glory, to have been cramped by General Clavering's moderating majority, or the self-denying resolutions of a secret committee—Seraje-ud-Dowla would probably have had ample cause to expatiate on the disinterested policy and unprecedented moderation of the British conqueror, but he would certainly have thought them much too sublime for imitation. Nor, indeed, would the treaty of Illahabad now exist to be held up by the committee as the

the model of political forbearance, and as the necessary boundary of future exertion. For by what right could Clive make treaties fword in hand at Illahabad? What plea of self-defence could our armies urge for paffing the Mahra ta ditch? —Entrenched behind that formidable bulwark, they fhould *there* have ftudied " *the maintenance of an inviolable character for mo-" deration, good faith, and a fcrupulous regard to " treaty, as the SIMPLE grounds on which the Britifh " governments fhould have endeavoured to eftablifh " an influence fuperior to that of other Europeans " over the minds of the native powers of India." His Highnefs the nabob Wawlaw Jaw would not, at this inftant, have ceafed to deplore the inefficacy of thefe *fimple grounds of influence*, had we relied on *them* for his eftablifhment on the mufnud of the Carnatic, and had we always refolutely refufed to " † interfere as " a party in the domeftic or national quarrels of the " country powers." — And, at this prefent hour, from our mouldering battlements of Fort St. George, (if the French had deemed it too defpicable an acquifition for themfelves,) and from the extenfive precincts of the Bound-hedge, we might have viewed, without concern, the fuccefsful ftruggles of ambition, or the ravages of increafing defolation —happy to procure a fcanty fupply of provifions, and a refufe of rotten goods for an occafional cargo, whenever a ftraggling peafant or pedlar fhould think us worth his notice, or the fhort intervals of peace freed him from danger. For the example of Mr. Dupleix, to which we ought gratefully to afcribe the firft hint of our territorial acquifitions in India, would have made little impreffion on the inflexible *moderation* of that triumvirate which prefided at the treaty of Poorunder.

It is humbly prefumed that *moderation, juftice, good*

---

* Fifth refolution.
† Third refolution.

faith,

faith, and all other virtues are of a very different nature in morality and in politics. In the former they are univerſal and unchangeable; in the latter, relative and reciprocal, and the terms of their definitions conſequently temporary and local. Thus *that* which is to-day *politically* moderate, may be to-morrow puſillanimous, and perhaps was inſolent yeſterday: A demand, which would be weakneſs at Fort William, is extravagance at Fort Malborough. — Moral virtues exiſt independent of intereſt, or of ſucceſs; both of which are eſſential to the merits of all political exertion. Political virtue does not teach us to offer the left cheek when the right has already been aſſaulted, but to repel violence by violence: and indeed the balance of national power is nothing but the perpetual ſyſtem of oppoſition ariſing from the action and reaction of claſhing parties, as the exact counterpoiſe of the centripetal and centrifugal forces neceſſarily produces reſt.

Under a ſenſe of this natural diſtinction between the moral and political το καλον, we can but cordially conſent to the commendatory part of the learned Lord's *firſt reſolution*, which ſanctions the treaty of Illahabad. In the eye of mere abſtracted morality *that* treaty could never be juſt, or moderate, or exemplary: as it reduced to our ſubjection ten millions of people, over whom we had not the ſhadow of pretence to reign; and as it obliged a vanquiſhed prince to cede to us, what he had neither option to refuſe, nor means to beſtow. But the meaſure was politically good, and expediency ſtampt a merit on its articles. —So far, therefore, we are agreed. But the *prohibitions* of any future enlargement of dominion, which are *there* pointedly brought to notice, and which, in fact, furniſh the baſis for all the cenſure which breathes in the following reſolutions, demand a ſhort arreſt of judgment. They were *certainly* moderate: we may doubt if they were politic. Perhaps too they were juſt; but they are at leaſt diametrically oppoſite

to

to the spirit of that system which dictated the treaty of Illahabad. Yet the resolution conveys an implied approbation of all our territorial acquisitions previous to that period. As if at that inftant, and at Illahabad only, *moderation, juftice*, and *good faith* had firft ftarted into exiftence: and as if the prohibitory condemnations of conqueft, &c. iffued by the Directors at that period, had not arifen from the obvious principle of momentary extacy on the prodigious ftroke they had juft made: and perhaps from that over-abundant caution, which a fudden tranfition from fcanty mediocrity to unexpected wealth is generally found to infpire.

The truth is, the Directors at the moment of their Bengal acquifitions, and for fome time after, were fo dazzled with the magnitude of the poffeffion, as to imagine it adequate to the relief of all poffible exigencies, and what no future probable advantage could ever compenfate for the rifk of lofing. Long experience, and the inceffant demands of the miniftry at home, have fince opened their eyes:—but, could they have gained (as they undoubtedly *have* gained by this time) a territorial fupport for the neceffary eftablifhment of Bombay, they would again, with pleafure, iffue forth *prohibitory condemnations of all fchemes of conqueft and enlargement of dominion*. (With a tacit referve probably for fuch fettlements, either now exifting, or hereafter to exift, as may require territorial fupport.)

The original fource of all our profperity in India has arifen, by an unforefeen chain of events, from unavoidable competition in trade; and it is by trade only that our Afiatic poffeffions are made productive in Europe. Our great rivals in commerce the Dutch have enjoyed undifturbed for more than a century and a half, that very valuable branch of merchandize which they had chofen for themfelves as the grand object of all their oriental fchemes. Vigorous and well-timed efforts might perhaps even now produce as favourable an event for ourfelves. Could we but

fall

fall on some simple and permanent plan for the good administration of our Asiatic possessions, could we, with double the mercantile abilities of the Dutch, be content to imitate their phlegm,—there is no present political impossibility why Great Britain should not exclusively furnish Europe with the muslins and callicoes of India, while Holland exclusively distributes its nutmegs and cloves.

But, however specious or practicable this idea of a monopoly of Indian manufactures may appear, there is no reason to suppose the plan ever to have been systematically adopted by the court of Directors, nor their conquests to have been pushed to an extravagant extent on this all-grasping, though mercantile principle. They have never appeared to stretch their ambition beyond objects, of which the attainment was equally obvious and necessary: and for this purpose have constantly expressed their paternal wish to provide something more than a precarious and eleemosynary subsistance for one of their earliest scyons, Bombay. The fortress of Bassein, and the islands of Salsette and Caranja, are the arms without which Bombay is but a barren trunk. The Portuguese once possessed them all, by the only title which was then, or will ever be, valid in politics, the tenure of the sword. From *them* Bombay came into our hands by cession (far be it from me to say we became receivers of stolen goods), and its appendages were wrested from them long after by the Mahrattas, *vi et armis*: from whom we have ever since wished to gain them on any terms: by composition,--by treaty,--by purchase,--and have, at length, procured them nearly by the means which they employed to get them from the Portuguese. The troubles of the Mahratta state gave grounds for hopes of every advantage. So distracted have been the councils of that nation for some years, so divided their chiefs, so fluctuating the authority, that the ruling power was hardly ever six months without a revolution. The seeds of contention were sown in the very principles of the government, and would long ago have ripened in our favour, were it not, that those *ministers*, as they are called, had discernment enough to return the observation on our Councils: and to place all their own hopes of security in the want of harmony among those whom they have chosen to style the *English chiefs*.

However, the infractions of the Poorunder treaty (even supposing them mutual) imposed the necessity of fresh negociation, and the indulgent reception which the French experienced at Poonah demanded the most effectual interposition; and it was happy, that, by the absolute defection of one of those two only ‡ ministers who had signed the Poorunder treaty, we were released in a great measure from all attention to it. *Then* it was that Mr. Hastings, (who, after spending several years at Calcutta, well knew the fatal effects of that continual drain of specie which the exigencies of Bombay caused from Bengal, who knew intimately the sentiments of his employers on this head, and who felt the critical coincidence of the present circumstances,) stepped forward with that vigour and promptitude of decision which distinguishes the sound statesman from the mere minister; and, by a measure worthy of Clive himself, almost fixed the very inconstancy of fortune. Even the natives of India were impressed with the highest astonishment at the boldness of the attempt to march an army from Calpee to Bombay. Mr. Francis opposed it, (the Report overflows with enumerations of his objections), and his opposition betrays the strongest symptoms of timidity and alarm. He constantly *fears where no fear is*; and in every step of the march * " thinks the detachment incapable of
" surmounting the dangers and difficulties of a fur-
" ther progress towards Bombay, and therefore ear-
" nestly recommends its immediate recall : *notwith-*
" *standing the avowed discredit which would thereby fall*

---

* Sixth report p. 8.   ‡ Sicca Ram Baboo.

" *upon*

" upon the wisdom of our councils and the power of our
" arms." Luckily enough for the credit both of our
councils and our arms these convulsions of timorous
apprehension were suffered to work themselves off, in
the feminine effusions of the tongue; and Mr.
Francis's political hysteric was at length effectually
relieved by the certainty of Col. Goddard's safe arrival at Surat.

All extensive territorial possession, particularly on a
continent, implies the necessity of political connexions. The moment our India Company had acquired the provinces of Bengal, Bahar, and Orissa, it
became necessarily linked in a certain degree with the
surrounding provinces, and in general with the powers
of India. But as these powers must at all times be
jealous of each other, and were frequently engaged in
actual hostilities, it might not always be in the power
of our Company (as one member of this grand body)
to stand neuter, and it might sometimes be serviceable
to take a decided part. Our grand difficulty lay in the
choice of the connexions to be formed; for the existence of *some* connexions, and therefore the necessity of
a choice, cannot be disputed.

Mr. Hastings succeeded to the government of Bengal in February 1772, a period big with every possible
calamity. The Company which he served, laboured
under a most ruinous debt, and an utter want of resource. The country which he came to govern, was
just emerging from the desolation of a famine. The
neighbouring provinces viewed us with no very friendly
eye, and there were also many symptoms of probable
confusion in the interior parts of Hindostan. A retrenchment of all unnecessary expence, a provision of
additional means, the security of our frontier, and
the formation of a profitable alliance, were the immediate consequences of his accession to the chair:—the
first and second, by internal reform, and a withholding
of the king's ill-deserved tribute; the third and fourth,
by an alliance offensive and defensive with Sujah-ud-Dowla.

Dowla. The result of these decisive measures was a great accession of wealth, and the return of general prosperity. In the grand mass of political connexion, it is very possible to form offensive alliances, to interfere in national quarrels, and to profit by occasional acquisitions, without the smallest derogation from moderation, wisdom, and good faith. The same prudence which obliges a merchant in pursuit of the immediate advantage of his *house*, to enter into a competition of trade, and to divert to his own coffers profits which originally flowed in other channels, will authorize in the politician an attempt to extend, by all fair and justifiable pretexts, the influence of his own nation in competition with that of other rival nations. Acting on this general principle of political good faith, Mr. Hastings, in his connexions and negotiations with the powers of India, has *always* contrived to turn the scale of advantage on the side of his employers. Things were precisely in this predicament, when General Clavering, with a Majority of the Supreme Council, arrived in Bengal. On the north, they found a part of our army engaged with that of the Vizier, our ally (and a very profitable one), in the reduction of a province deemed by him to be in actual rebellion. Our troops were paid by the Vizier, and our assistance had been purchased by a very large pecuniary compensation. The political justice of the war rested with its Principal. Had he engaged in it, and conquered, without our aid, *we* had no right to interpose as umpires in the dispute, nor to share in the advantages of the conquest. Had he fought, and been vanquished, the necessity of securing our own frontier would eventually have forced us to join him, or lie open to other invasions from the Mahrattas. So that, in fact, we, as having no right to controul the actions of our immediate neighbour, the Vizier, could not bind him down to a peace—as having no political, nor so much as commercial or vicinal, intercourse with the Rohillas, could not risk even a
coolness.

coolness, much less a dispute with him at our doors for their protection. And we had but the alternative of being exposed to every possible inconvenience on the close of the war, or to interfere in its successful accomplishment on the side of the Vizier. Necessity, I repeat it, would in the end have driven us to solicit a second alliance with him, had we at that time, by a pointed refusal to join in his measures, interrupted the good harmony of the first.—We met his proposals, and ensured the most striking benefits to both parties. On the western side of India, the presidency of Bombay had but lately, by a sudden effort of vigour, secured possession of the islands of Salsette and Caranja—not indeed without violence, but yet with a plausible pretext—and the acquisition had been ratified by the approbation of the Court of Directors, who had long wished to obtain them on any terms. The result, however, of the seizure was a war with the Mahrattas, from whom we had taken them; and which (though it had not been attended with uninterrupted success) gave sufficient hopes of a fortunate and even of a speedy termination.

The vigorous prosecution of our measures had already succeeded in Rohilcund, and on those in operation on the Bombay side depended almost all the future prosperity of the Company in that quarter; and they even nearly promised success at the period when the new Majority of the Supreme Council entered on Indian affairs.——Wholly occupied with the wish to drive Mr. Hastings from his government, and anxious to establish their own character on the ruin of that of their rival, they had no means left but by a strong opposition to all the leading principles of his administration. Hence, as the nice management of political connexion, and the critical exertion of well-directed force, had already, in Mr. Hastings's hands, produced the most important consequences; and as he was too strongly entrenched on *that* ground to be displaced by any manœuvre of chicane, the only method by which they could possibly hope to rise to notice, was the adoption of a system which should diametrically oppose the plans of the General. Hence our brigade was recalled from Rohilcund with a precipitancy which even alarmed the Company at home: a peace was instantly sollicited with the Mahrattas, on humiliating terms; or on any terms. Our allies were taught that the English had now circumscribed their politics as well as their arms by an immoveable barrier: that neither the importance of *their* occasions, nor the prospect of *our own* aggrandizement, could ever again induce us to draw the sword. Our enemies were instructed, that we sate quietly at home to receive them, however hostile might be their professions, or well-appointed their force: that, however *unjust*, *faithless*, or *immoderate* their demands might prove, Our's were now no more. It is well that the Mahrattas forgot at that moment their pretensions to the Chout; and that the King neglected to require restitution of his provinces, under failure of the treaty of Illahabad. Had Sujah-ud-Dowla lived, *He* too would probably have had some claims to make on our moderation. *He* would little have brooked to *pay* troops which he was not permitted to *employ*. *He* would have sought for more spirited and less scrupulous allies—perhaps have recollected that he had once been formidable even to the English. But *He* died in time, and left a son weak enough to imitate our treaty of Poorunder, by that which he submitted to at Fyzabad.

It is from the moment that the Supreme Council in Bengal assumed an unlimited controul over the politics of all the Company's settlements, it is from the spirit of that opposition which dictated and concluded the pusillanimous treaty of Poorunder, that we may date the first avowed doctrine of chimerical neutrality and mere passive self-defence. It was that first partial sacrifice of the Company's interests in pursuit of private ends, which has laid the foundation for the exaggerated pretensions and extravagant presumption of the country powers. It is to this source, and perhaps to this alone, that we should in truth and candour impute the troubles in the Carnatic, and the war with the

Mah-

Mahrattas. And, if we would preserve the footing we still hold in those very distant regions,---if we would guarantee to the Company and to the Nation those ineſtimable advantages which our Indian settlements produce,---it can only be effected by the proper delegation of diſcretionary powers, and by the ſelection of ſuch agents as may be entitled to a very liberal ſhare of public confidence. Poſitive and unconditional orders will never operate with proſperous effect to the extent of half the globe.

In the breaſts of thoſe, whom the acknowledged candour and applauſive ſtyle of the firſt reſolution has impreſſed with ſome degree of conſideration for the zeal and abilities heretofore exerted by the court of directors, in the ſervice and for the advantage of its conſtituents, the ſubſequent reſolutions cannot fail to excite a little ſurpriſe.—What an extraordinary Change!—How ſhall we account for it! What? the ſame court which ſo lately and ſo allowably profited by the treaty of Illahabad, condemned merely for *turning a few Rupees* at the treaty of Benaras!!! But by the latter the Rohillas were exterminated.—And who were the Rohillas, that they ſhould eſcape political juſtice for their own atrocious uſurpations, and denial of ſtipulated tribute?—But the Rohillas were not actuated by the moderating principles of the treaty of Iſſahabad, and therefore conquered where they could, and had a right to every advantage of temporary ſucceſs.—Be it ſo—But their neighbours had alſo in their turn a right to ſecure their own tranquillity,—or to proſecute any other uſeful political purpoſe at the expence of the intruding Rohillas. Of thoſe who ſurvived their ſeveral defeats, the greater part returned to thoſe impenetrable hills from whence they had deſcended in ſearch of plunder, and the reſt found a quiet aſylum and even a liberal ſupport in the very dominions of the prince whom they had grievouſly offended.——The much-arraigned and ill-underſtood Rohilla war, after having cauſed almoſt as great an effuſion of ink as of blood, is now to be deciſively

cisively condemned.—Still the reasons urged by the late president and council of Bengal for the commencement of that war, the pleas of necessity and others, which they have since furnished in defence of the measure, are not done away in the report. If we look into the appendix, we may perhaps be bewildered by the sophistry of General Clavering's majority—but by no means convinced by their arguments. The contrast of praise and blame on the conduct of the court of directors, which forms so striking a feature on the face of the resolutions, however ably and spiritedly drawn, almost amounts to a distinction without a difference. The directors, probably, as little deserved applause for ratifying the treaty of Illahabad, as they now merit censure for having admitted that settled at Benaras, or for wishing to improve the treaty of Poorunder.—In either case, they seem to have acted perfectly in character, conscientiously to have discharged the duties of their appointment, and fulfilled their delegated trust, by consulting, to the utmost of their abilities, the grand interests of their principals. They were to be guided in all their operations by the original charters of the company, none of which contain a syllable of that forbearing system of policy which is now recommended. By the charter, they may build forts and acquire lands to an indefinite extent. It has been amply demonstrated, that their acquisitions, both now and heretofore, have been for the purpose of immediate self-defence, or the supply of necessary emergencies—nor is there in the Report, or elsewhere, any *proof* of wanton violence or injustice, that can be applied to any particular period. On the contrary, it will be found, that as the pretence for our first expulsion from Calcutta by the nabob Seraj-ud-Doula, was the protection † we unwarrantably extended to one of his rebellious subjects; so one original cause ‡ of the

---

† See Vansittart's Narrative, Hollwell, Orme, &c.
‡ Fifth report, p. 27.

Mahratta

Mahratta war was the assistance afforded to Ragoba; who, from having been actual regent* of the Mahratta empire, was thrust from his dignity, and treated as a rebel, by those who in a violent manner succeeded to his place—And that, in a second instance, the act which furnished the principal pretext for the revival of the same war, subsequent to the treaty of Poorunder, was the same protection again afforded by us to the same Ragoba.

But our refusal to deliver up † Kissen Doss, at the repeated demands of his rightful sovereign, eventually produced the conquest of Bengal, Bahar, and Orissa—and those acquisitions belong to the treaty of Illahabad, consequently are consistent with wisdom, moderation, and justice. Our obstinacy in refusing to sacrifice Ragoba to his revengeful rivals Nana Furnese or Tuckajee Holkar, has certainly by this time ensured us the much-desired possession of Bassein and Salsette. That they might, indeed, have been ours long before, a candid perusal of the fifth report will hardly fail to evince—had General Clavering's majority taken another twelvemonth to learn their political alphabet, and had not the sanguine efforts of Mr. Hastings for this valuable addition to the property of his masters, produced from the opposition that scandalous dereliction of all their dearest and best interests, the Poorunder treaty. But our late successes are too modern not to be deemed usurpations. They fall within the denunciations of the first six resolutions, as they are most indubitably not " founded on the princi- " ple of the treaty of Illahabad." But these two bug-bear treaties are for ever in our way. Let us once for all dismiss them fairly. That of Illahabad was undoubtedly a wise and a politic measure, and at the same time wonderfully advantageous—but, for my soul, I never could discover wherein consisted its *mo-*

---

* Fifth report, p. 26.
† Orme's history, 2d vol. pages 49, 50.

deration

deration. Lord Clive himself would probably have blushed at so extraordinary a piece of flattery. Of the treaty of Poorunder nothing can be said, but that it was in every respect the reverse of the former; and therefore we will allow it to have been as moderate as even Mahratta impudence could well demand. We might at least have expected to see it readily and satisfactorily ratified. But the Poona Durbar had felt our political pulse, and found that an internal disorder preyed on our vitals, and benumbed all the nerves of our dominion. This treaty, therefore (infamous as it was), they delayed to execute; and that very delay in some degree saved its credit, by contributing most Inconceivably to the somewhat more disgraceful convention of Worgaum.

On the whole, it is most earnestly entreated, that a strict attention to the immediate circumstances which led to the appointment of the secret committee, as well as a considerate review of 5th and 6th reports, may precede any opinion on the resolutions. In England, all public measures (if unsuccessful) occasion an immediate alarm. "Sacrifice of national honour"—"contempt and disobedience of orders"—"wilful neglect and corrupt practices"—are loudly imputed to the unfortunate men who devised, or who were to have executed, the defeated plan. We institute tedious enquiries when we should urge instant and vigorous exertions. The Athenians idly disputed for the palm of eloquence, till Philip was at their very doors—but the Romans, when severely beaten by Pyrrhus, would not so much as listen to any terms of accommodation until the conqueror had left Italy. In the present case, while some of the ablest members of our legislature have been anxiously investigating the causes of the wars with the Mahrattas and with Hyder Ally; and laboriously sifting, from bushels of dusty records, a few choice grains of truth and common sense—a Coote has driven Hyder for ever from the Carnatic, and a Goddard has turned the scale of negotiation most

decidedly

decidedly in our favour with the Mahrattas. It cannot but be remembered, under what gloomy apprehensions the honourable Committee took its seat. Let it be remembered, in how glorious a reverse it is now about to close its reports.

The learned lord, to whose undoubted abilities the compilation of those reports must ever do honour, in his prefatory speech to the consequent resolutions, has so pointedly, so solicitously referred to the reports themselves for the foundation of all judgment—has so warmly recommended a careful comparison of each line and word of the resolutions with the original report, out of which they profess to grow—that no weightier arguments need be urged, or can be added, in effectual persuasion of this necessary purpose. If the preceding sheets do not entirely coincide with the opinions deduced by the learned lord from his own statement of the case, it is with the utmost deference, and in consequence of the closest application to the *whole matter* of the 6th report, and to part of the 5th, that they are here submitted to the public. The comparison so repeatedly urged by the very learned and respectable compiler of both papers has been followed up with the coolest reflection; and the result of it is also here most respectfully subjoined, in the form of short observations on each resolution.

RESOLUTIONS read Monday, April 15, 1782.	OBSERVATIONS.
1. That the orders of the court of directors of the East India company, which have conveyed to their servants abroad a prohibitory condemnation of all schemes of conquest and enlargement of dominion, by prescribing certain	The orders of the court of directors, founded on the treaty of Illahabad, most certainly conveyed a clear prohibition of enlarging our dominions on that side of India where the treaty took its rise—and the line was in after-times

Resolutions.	Observations.

tain rules and boundaries for the operation of their military force, and enjoining a strict adherence to a system of defence upon the principle of the treaty of Illahabad, were founded no less in wisdom and policy, than in justice and moderation.

2. That every transgression of those orders, without evident necessity, by any of the several British governments in India, has been highly reprehensible, and has tended in a chief degree to weaken the force and influence, and to diminish the resources, of the company in those parts.

3. That every interference as a party in the domestic or national quarrels of the country powers, and all new engagements with them in offensive alliance, have been wisely and providently forbidden by the Company in their commands to their administrations in India.

4. That every unnecessary or avoidable deviation from those well-advised rules, should be followed with very severe reprehension

times precisely drawn by the general limitation which confined our armies to our side of the Caramnassa. The expressions, indeed, of the court of directors to their servants abroad, seem to have been too general, and to comprehend *all* their settlements;—but the whole tenor of their conduct from that period, the whole spirit of their correspondence, shews that this prohibition never was meant to extend to Bombay, for which settlement they have incessantly repeated their wishes to procure an adequate territorial establishment.

The first grand consideration of the court of directors must necessarily have been, to promote by all means (consistent with the rules of trade, the powers of their charter, and the laws of nations) the immediate interests of their employers, according to the several exigencies of the times. In their days of prosperity, they procured the treaty of Illahabad: in the moment of dejection, they were saddled

| RESOLUTIONS. | OBSERVATIONS. |

sion and punishment for it, as an instance of wilful disobedience of orders, and as tending to disturb and destroy that state of tranquillity and peace with all their neighbours, the preservation of which has been recommended as the first principle of policy to the British governments in India.

5. That the maintenance of an inviolable character for moderation, good faith, and scrupulous regard to treaty, ought to have been the simple grounds on which the British governments should have endeavoured to establish an influence superior to that of other Europeans over the minds of the native powers in India; and that the danger and discredit arising from the forfeiture of this pre-eminence, could not be compensated by the temporary success of any plan of violence or injustice.

6. That as any essential failure in the executive conduct of the supreme council or presidencies would make them justly liable to the most serious

saddled with that of Poorunder. Like sensible men, they have stuck to the first bargain, which was clearly profitable; and, like good merchants, they have shifted the latter from their shoulders the instant that a flaw in the agreement, or a non-performance of the conditions, afforded them a plea on commercial grounds.

The company, as a trading body, must naturally place the first pre-eminence of a merchant in the *good faith* of his compting-house, and the *honor* of his bills. No *danger*, no *discredit*, could more immediately operate on such a body, than the forfeiture of this pre-eminence.

The pretensions of the Company, like the hagglings of a dealer, though dictated by self-interest, have not been deficient in the common and customary appeals to reason, justice, and propriety.

RESOLUTIONS.	OBSERVATIONS.
serious animadversions of their superiors; so should any relaxation, without sufficient cause, in these principles of good government, on the part of the Directors themselves, bring upon them, in an heavier degree, the resentment of the legislative power of their country, which alone can interpose an effectual correction to the general misrule.	
7. That the conduct of the Company and their servants in India to the King and Nudjiff Cawn, with respect to the tribute payable to the one, and the stipend to the other, and with respect to the transfer of the provinces of Corah and Illahabad to the Vizier, was contrary to policy and good faith; and that such wise and practicable measures should be adopted in future as may tend to redeem the national honour, and recover the confidence and attachment of the princes of India.	1. If the *Company* be censured for withholding the king's tribute and Nudjiff Cawn's stipend, the Company's servants are *ipso facto* acquitted. 2. If it be meant to "*redeem the national honour,*" by paying up the arrears of tribute; or even (which may perhaps be all that is here implied) by remitting it regularly *in future* from Bengal; the treaty of Illahabad will soon cease to be popular. 3. We guaranteed Corah and Illahabad to the king, for himself, with an express stipulation that he should reside there. We resumed them, when we found he was determined
8. That	mined

RESOLUTIONS.	OBSERVATIONS.
	mined to quit all connexion with us, to undertake a knight-errant expedition to Dehli, and to give up those provinces to the Mahrattas. The King must long have been heartily disgusted with the treaty of Illahabad; and, were we now to pay the tribute originally agreed by it, he would probably employ the money in armaments to disturb us in the peaceable enjoyment of its other articles.
8. That too strong a confirmation cannot be given to the sentiments and resolutions of the court of directors, and of the court of proprietors of the East India company, in comdemnation of the Rohilla war: that the conduct of the President and Select Committee of Bengal appears, in almost every stage of it, to have been biassed by an interested partiality to the vizier, to transgress their own as well as the company's positive and repeated regulations and orders: that the extermination of the Rohillas was not necessary for the recovery of forty lacks of	1 The court of directors and the court of proprietors, did, in December 1775, express a disapprobation of the principles of the Rohilla war; but they never thought of refunding the price of our assistance. The fact is, they condemned the measure, because they feared it might afford a dangerous precedent under a less able governor. They also positively disclaimed all suspicion of corrupt motives in their president Warren Hastings, esq. without proof. No proof of *interested* partiality to the vizier is to be found in the report: and, as the character of a man of

RESOLUTIONS.	OBSERVATIONS.
of rupees; and that, if it was expedient to make their country a barrier against the Marattas, there is reason to believe that this might have been affected by as easy and by a less iniquitous interference of the government of Bengal, which would at the same time have preserved the dominion to the rightful owners, and exhibited an attentive example of justice as well as policy to all India.	of honour is infinitely more wounded by the mere imputation of criminal self-interest than the full conviction of erroneous judgment, we will (till some *proof* shall authorize the present reading) venture at all events to substitute the word *political* for *interested*, previous to partiality. It will then stand, that it might appear to Mr. Hastings *politically right* to assist Soujah'udDowla in the conquest of the Rohillas, and to the Committee's cool deliberation it appears *politically wrong*. Secondly, granting that the Vizier had a demand on the Rohillas for forty lacks of rupees; if by their pertinacious refusal to pay a just debt, they obliged him to recur to forcible means, and then were invincibly resolved to perish in resistance to his arms, their extermination does really appear to have been necessary for the recovery of these forty lacks. Just as a bailiff, in the ordinary course of duty, may be reduced to the necessity of knocking down, maiming, or otherwise ill treating a refractory

Resolutions.	Observations.
	refractory debtor, who opposes the execution of a writ. Thirdly, if there were more modes than one by which the Rohilla country could be made a barrier against the Mahrattas (in which case assertion must not stand in the place of truth), an error in the choice of those modes does not imply any iniquitous interference. — But it is most certain that the dominion of that county could *not possibly be preserved* to the *rightful* owners, without previously dispossessing the Rohillas, whose usurpation had not even reached the period usually required to ascertain a right of prescription.
9. That the company's servants in their presidency of Bombay, were guilty of very notorious instances of disobedience to the orders of their employers, as well in the proceedings against the nabob of Broach, as in the commencement of the Marratta war, by the seizure of the islands of Salsette and Caranja.	1. The company's wish to acquire some territorial supports for their settlements on the western side of India, is of public and undoubted notoriety. The company's servants, however they might originally exceed the commands of their masters in the seizure of Salsette, &c. yet are allowed to have received the full remission of their sin, in the subsequent countenance and sanction afforded
10. That it appears that the court of directors made use of very strong expressions,	

(32)

| RESOLUTIONS. | OBSERVATIONS. |

tions, to communicate their ~~wish of~~ acquiring thofe iflands, and the fortrefs of Baffein; and although in the month of April 1775, previous to the receipt of intelligence that Salfette was taken, they very explicitly confined their fervants at Bombay to meafures of negociation, as the only means they authorized for making the acquifition; yet after knowledge of the event, they do not feem to have fignified any difpleafure at the tranfaction, or any farther anxiety than about the prefervation of the conqueft : and that the court of directors in this inftance gave countenance and fanction to the very meafure they had themfelves fo pointedly condemned, and are therefore fo far chargeable with the refponfibility of it.

- 11. That in forming an offenfive alliance with Ragoba, the government of Bombay violated the orders of the company againft any con-

afforded to the meafure by the court of directors; therefore are no longer objects of cenfure. ——
2. Ragoba was firft regent, and afterward Pefhwa of the Mahratta empire, and, for aught that is *proved* in the report, had as much right to enter into treaties, as his majefty Shah Allum himfelf; and had, at one time, much more power to enforce them. The company's prohibitions of offenfive alliances, &c. clearly related to the ftate of their affairs on the other fide of India. With refpect to their weftern purfuits, they only * *rather wifh they could be obtained by purchafe than war*; and, confining their views to the acquifition of Salfette and Baffein, &c. caution their fervants; † *in all their treaties, negociations, and military operations, to be ever watchful to obtain them.* Their fervants, in confequence, made a *treaty* with Ragoba, by which they were

* 5 Report, page 60. Extract of General Letter to Bombay, 18 March, 1768.
† General Letter to Bombay, 31 March, 1769.

RESOLUTIONS.	OBSERVATIONS.
connections of that nature, and against any interference in the quarrels of the native powers: that they undertook, without a certainty of an adequate revenue, or a sufficient military force, and without proper communication with the superior government upon which they were to depend for sanction and support, to place that chief on the musnud at Poonah, and thereby to involve themselves in a war with the ruling ministers of the Maratta state; while Ragoba himself was not in the mean time able to give the company secure possession of any of the grants he had made to them for the purchase of their assistance.	were formally ceded to us; ‡ *negotiated* at several times with the other Mahratta chiefs for the delivery of them, and have at last obtained possession by *military operations*.
12. That the measures taken by the majority, which then consisted of Messrs. Clavering, Monson, and Frances, in the government of Bengal, for the restoration of peace, were wise and just in their principle, and conformable to the spirit of the company's orders, notwithstanding	The method of interference adopted by General Clavering and his majority in the business of Bombay, was abrupt, impolitic, personal, and disadvantageous to their employers.—Abrupt, in that, on their arrival at Bengal, they proceeded to a decision on the state of affairs, befor

‡ See 5 Report, page 74, 16 and 17 lines.

(34)

RESOLUTIONS.	OBSERVATIONS.
withstanding that their method of interference was not afterwards approved of by the court of directors. 13. That the terms of the treaty concluded by colonel Upton at Poorunder, in the beginning of March 1776, were honourable and advantageous to the company; when the circumstances of the rise and progress of the war, the want of resources for carrying it on, the state of the contending parties, the instructions of the superior council, and the general sentiments of the company, are attended to. 14. That the perseverance of the superior government, in directing the execution of the articles of accommodation, was judicious and commendable, notwithstanding that the presidency of Bombay protested against them, as inadequate and highly injurious to the reputation, honour, and interests of the company: and that the court of directors, in their	before they could possibly become in any degree masters of the subject:—impolitic, in that, by the violent change introduced by their system, they § betrayed the weakness and disunion of our government to all India:—personal, in presuming to give ‖ *private verbal instructions* to Colonel Upton, which must necessarily tend to alarm the Governor-general, and to lower him in the eyes of the Company's immediate servants, as well as their allies and connexions: — disadvantageous, in as much as there is reason to suppose, that we might have retained, from that moment, " *all the ceded territories (except Bassein)*," they being then in our possession; and that the blood and treasure, which have since been lavished in the struggle for them, might have been entirely saved, † *had Colonel Upton but shewn a firm determination not to part with them.*

§ 5 Report, page 82.
‖ 5 Report, pages 88, 89.
† 5 Report, page 82.

RESOLUTIONS.	OBSERVATIONS.
their letter of the 15th December 1775, which reached Calcutta on 1st July 1776, declared their intentions of keeping all territories and possessions ceded to the company by the treaty concluded with Ragoba.	
15. That the president and council of Bombay, in granting an asylum to Ragoba after the conclusion of the treaty of Poorunder, did not thereby commit any direct infringement on the stipulations of that treaty, provided they had taken no other offensive measure in support of his cause: and it appears, that this conduct coincided with the sentiments and instructions of the court of Directors, who made the personal safety of Ragoba one of the conditions of their acquiescence in the treaty of Poorunder.	The Governor-general is here charged with shewing a strong tendency for the renewal of the Mahratta war, after it had ceased by the treaty of Poorunder.———Undoubtedly, the Governor-general had always opposed that treaty; the Council of Bombay had protested against it; and the Court of Directors disapproved of it. But, in fact, the Governor-general's measures had *no tendency to a renewal of the war:* his words and his wishes were alike for peace.—But, as the terms of the treaty were still unfulfilled, he thought himself entitled to insist on the *definitive execution* of them. The instructions to Bombay, said to contain a virtual encouragement as well as precise authority † " to form
16. That it appears that the Court of Directors, by their letters to Bengal of 5th February, and to Bombay of 16th April 1777, manifested some dissatisfaction at the terms	

† 19 Resolut.

RESOLUTIONS.	OBSERVATIONS.
terms of the treaty of Poorunder, as it had not procured for the Company the surrender of Bassein, and gave very strong encouragement to both Presidencies, to seize the slightest pretence of provocation from the Ministers to renew their engagement with Ragoba.	form a new alliance with Ragoba, and to engage with him in any scheme they should deem expedient and safe for retrieving his affairs," wear a very different aspect, when contrasted with the hypothetical proposition immediately preceding the close of the paragraph.
17. That it appears that the propositions of the Governor-general, recorded on the 26th January 1778, were evidently founded on these sentiments of the Court of Directors, contained demands on the Maratta administration greatly exceeding the conditions of the treaty of Poorunder, and opened the first design of sending a detachment from Bengal to the Malabar coast.	‡ *If*, say the Governor-general and Council, the present or future members of the administration shall either directly infringe the treaty, *or* permit it to be infringed by persons acting under their authority, *or* shall refuse to fulfil the conditions of it, (then, and in that case only, is of necessity to be understood) we, *as authorized by the Company*, do invest you with authority to form a new alliance with Ragoba, &c.
18. That the resolution of the majority of the Supreme Council on the 2d February 1778, which by the death of Colonel Monson was now decided by the casting voice of the Governor general, had a strong tendency to a renewal	——To be sure, with great reason.—Were we not only to sit still under a treaty expressly declared to be *inadequate*, and *highly injurious to the reputation, honour, and interests of the Company*, but to submit

‡ 6 Report, page 10.

RESOLUTIONS.	OBSERVATIONS.
newal of the Maratta war; because it gave a sanction and confirmation to the resolution of the Bombay Council of the 10th and 12th December preceding, to co-operate with a confederacy of some of the Maratta Ministers, in carrying Ragoba to Poona. 19. That it appears that the Court of Directors in their letter of 4th July 1777, to the President and Council of Bombay, enjoined them to pay a strict adherence to the treaty of Poorunder; but gave them at the same time orders to obey the directions of the Superior Council, who were possessed of a discretionary licence to resume the cause of Ragoba; and that the proceedings of the Governor-general and Council, on the 23d March 1778, and the letter written in consequence, containing instructions to the administration at Bombay, amounted to a virtual encouragement, as well as authority to them, "to "form a new alliance "with	mit also with patience to every wanton violation or perverse misconstruction of that treaty?— 2. The resolution in favour of Ragoba had no necessary tendency to a renewal of the war. For, if, (* as was asserted) one of the ‡ two Mahratta ministers who had signed the treaty of Poorunder really encouraged a cooperation with Ragoba and the Bombay Council, there was great political probability, that our weight thrown into a cause already equally poised, would decidedly turn the scale; and it might also happen, that the party which proposed a change of measures by a coalition with us, might already possess such preponderance. The Poonah ministry might possibly have one general outline of action, without the unanimity of a British jury.

* 6 Report, page 6.   ‡ Sicca-Ram Baboo.

Resolutions.	Observations.
" with Ragoba, and to engage with him in any scheme they should deem expedient and safe for retrieving his affairs." 20. That it appears, that a French agent had been received at Poona, in the beginning of the year 1777, and that negociations were supposed to be thenceforward carried on between him and the Maratta government, of a tendency inimical to the British interests; that General Clavering had declared his opinion, "that all the acts of the Bombay presidency had been so manifestly hostile to the Maratta state, he was not surprized at their endeavour to form connections with the French, to protect themselves against such unfriendly and unjustifiable proceedings:" That Colonel Upton had ascribed to the Presidency of Bombay, the blame of delay and obstruction to the conclusion of the treaty; and had given his opinion, "That when all the conditions of it should be carried into execution,	The Mahrattas, as an independent power, would negotiate now, or at any other time, with the French, Portuguese, Dutch, or any other European nation which they thought could be serviceable to their interests or their arms. Gen. Clavering's declared opinion, that a Minister from the Superior Council residing at Poonah would preclude all the possibility of French intrigue, does no great honour to his politics. Information had at that moment been received by Mr. Hastings, through several channels, that Choul was to be ceded to the French, that a body of troops was actually ready at the island Mauritius to take possession of it, and that the Court of Versailles had definitively resolved to attack us in India. All this can be *proved*. General Clavering was not infallible.

Resolutions.	Observations.
" execution, the French intrigues at the Maratta Durbar would no longer give any alarm; and that if a Minister from the Superior Council was sent to reside there, which the Peshwa and the Ministers had ever requested, the interest of the Company with the Poona Government would be secured against every attempt to supplant it."	
21. That it appears that the Governor-general on the 1st June 1778, professed his resolution of supporting Ragoba, as a mere instrument for defeating the projects of the French, and of giving security and permanency to the peace of the settlement of Bombay: That on receipt of accounts from Europe, of a rupture with France, the majority of the board, on the motion of the Governor-general, resolved upon a deputation to Berar, to form an offensive alliance with the Raja.	The Governor-general never was hearty in the cause of Ragoba—He used him as an instrument recommended by his masters, until, on the news of a rupture with France, the necessity of acquiring, if possible, a powerful Indian ally, superseded the duty of protecting Ragoba.
22. That	Whether

(40)

RESOLUTIONS.

22. That any support of Ragoba, inconsistent with the treaty of Poorunder, does not appear to have been so necessary or advisable a means for defeating the supposed projects of the French in conjunction with the Marattas, as to risk the certain expence and uncertain event of such an undertaking.

23. That it does not appear to have been a necessary or advisable means for defeating the supposed projects of the French, to depart from the settled maxim of the Company's policy, and to hazard the consequence of an offensive alliance with the Raja of Berar, for the avowed purpose of recovering for him the conquests made by the Nizam, and of uniting the dangerous powers of the Maratta empire under one active command.

OBSERVATIONS.

Whether the support of Ragoba as a means to counteract French influence were necessary or advisable, must depend on the efficacy allowed to that influence. General Clavering, we see by the last resolution, to evade this consideration, only denied the existence of French influence; which events have amply refuted.

1. The Mahratta powers, united under one active command, are indisputably dangerous; but they are, for that simple reason, enabled to be serviceable. The Governor general's view at the moment of this proposition, was to secure an effective ally against the powers of France, which may also be pronounced somewhat dangerous, and might require to be well matched.

2. The offer of recovering for Moodajee Boosla the capture made on his dominions by Nizam Ally, was merely one of the grounds on which the Governor-general thought * it might be possible to enter

---

* 6 Report, page 18.

RESOLUTIONS.	OBSERVATIONS.
	enter into a negotiation with that Raja. He positively declared, that the measure, as it then stood, was purely defensive; and the hint seems to have been only thrown out as a lure to encourage the Raja to treat with us at all. Nothing in the report goes to prove that we must have pledged ourselves at all events to undertake a war against Nizam Ally.
24. That it appears that the Nizam, in the month of July 1778, warned the Governor-general, as he had before done the Governor of Madras, in the most unequivocal manner, of the nature of his connections with the Poona government, and of the hostile part which he should take against the Company, in consequence of the support they might give to the pretensions of Ragoba: And that it further appears, that he engaged to insist upon the execution of the treaty of Poorunder, and to take part with the Company against the Maratta ministers, if they should be found to give any	1. *Dolus an virtus, quis in hoste requirit?* It suited the Nizam's purpose of the moment to deny the existence of French influence at the Poonah Durbar, or at least to assert that he could and would render it ineffectual, &c. &c. with other magnificent bravadoes. But who can answer for the Nizam's sincerity? He appears to have acted from a rooted personal dislike to Ragoba.
	2. Whether so politic and so selfish a prince as Nizam Ally was quite candid in his offers, and whether an acceptance of those offers would have been a more wise, safe, and honourable plan of defence against the machinations of

RESOLUTIONS.	OBSERVATIONS.
any countenance or encouragement to the French.	of the French, than any other, is a doubt not entirely cleared up by any documents to be found in the report. Facts are unequivocal. We *have* defeated the French intrigues, and we have done it without the assistance, nay in the very teeth of the Nizam; who, after all his blusterings, seems to have acquiesced very quietly in the assurances of the Governor-general's pacific intentions.— Turn where we will to the records, we find the Governor-general an advocate for reasonable peace, but an utter stranger to the language of alarm or of submission.
25. That a more certain means of completing the stipulations of the treaty of Poorunder, and a more wise, safe, and honourable plan of defence against the machinations of the French, might have been effected at that period, than either an offensive alliance with the Raja of Berar, or any active inteference in favour of Ragonaut Row.	
26. That under all the circumstances of the times, it was not only unnecessary but impolitic, to take any measures conducive to a re-commencement of hostilities against the Marattas, without a certainty of the friendship and concurrence of Hyder Ally, and the effectual support of a powerful party in the Poona government; and that	The censurable part of the Mahratta war lies, it must be confessed, on the shoulders of the Bombay gentlemen;—but not for the protection extended to Ragoba, which had been thoroughly approved by their masters.

† 6 Report page 20.

Resolutions.	Observations.

that therefore, the resolutions of the President and Select Committee of Bombay, on the 21st July, and the conditional approbation sent by the superior board, on the 17th August 1778, were so far reprehensible.

27. That the proceedings and resolutions of the President and Majority of the Select Committee of Bombay, on the 12th October 1778, and the military operations undertaken in consequence of them, were rash, unauthorized, and impolitic, and therefore highly reprehensible; because the situation and circumstances of their own strength and resources, the uncertainty of support from the Bengal detachment, the improbability of any material aid from a party in favour of Ragoba, and his reluctant consent to the terms prescribed for his own conduct, concurred in rendering the expedition to Poona a very dangerous and unpromising enterprize.

28. That it appears, that the Court of Directors,

RESOLUTIONS.	OBSERVATIONS.
tors, in their letter of 27th May 1779, gave a warm approbation to the treaty and negociation formed with Ragoba, for the purpose of an expedition to Poona, and gave it a decisive preference over every connection with the Rajah of Berar, which might set aside or counteract it.	
29. That as well the undertaking as the failure of the expedition were attended with the most unfortunate and distressing circumstances for the Company's affairs; and that as the support of Ragoba had shaken the confidence of the native princes in our good faith, the defeat of the enterprize lessened their idea of our power, and that in consequence thereof, their inclinations and hopes were incited and encouraged to hostile opposition against us.	It no way appears, that the support of Ragoba had shaken the *general* confidence of the native princes in our good faith. Ragoba, who at last sought our protection, might, in his brighter days, have commanded our alliance. The Nizam was, indeed, offended at our interference, but merely on personal motives. The Poonah ministers were parties in the cause, and their assertions go for nothing. Apostacy of friends, and encouragement to enemies, is the necessary consequence of a defeat: a falling nation, like a falling minister, will be attacked from many an unexpected quarter.
30. That it appears, that another distressing con-	The subterfuge at Worgaum, like a later event of

RESOLUTIONS.	OBSERVATIONS.
consequence of the engagement with Ragoba, and the unfortunate issue of the expedition, was the necessity of having recourse to subterfuge at the time of the convention at Worgaum, and to subsequent disavowal by the Superior Council, to evade the performance of the articles of convention.	of the same kind at Jersey, was the result of momentary calamity in the course of war. That the engagement with Ragoba led to this misfortune, is very true—but not therefore criminal; for the same engagement might have set Ragoba on the Poonah musnud. This resolution therefore, considered abstractedly, goes no farther than simply to resolve that the Report is the Report———
31. That it appears that Sir Eyre Coote, in his letter of the 18th January 1779, condemned the conduct of the two Presidencies of Bengal and Bombay, and with good reason denounced the probable bad consequences of the expedition to Poonah, and of the march of the detachment "which was sent from Bengal at an immense expence, and could produce nothing but distress to the company, not to say dishonour to the nation, whether successful or not."	It is allowed that Sir Eyre Coote did express such opinions in his letters of 18 Jan. 1779. He has proved himself upon all occasions a most able and a most fortunate commander—but cannot here be exalted to a prophet. Indeed, so far as concerns the distress and dishonour brought on the company by the march to Poonah, he was right—for that march turned out unsuccessfully.—But the prophecy failed of its completion with respect to the Bengal detachment, which has already procured much territory and considerable revenue to the company,

32. That

Resolutions.	Observations.
	as well as the immediate distress occasioned by its expences; and which we do not find to have been concerned in any thing immediately or ultimately dishonourable to the company or the nation. The measure was bold and unprecedented—therefore it might be deemed alarming—Had it failed—the dishonour of its ill success would have fallen on him or them who adopted it. Events have crowned it with honour to all parties. In a general distribution the Madras government will naturally come in for its proportion.
32. That it appears that the president and select committee of Fort St. George, in their letter of 7th February 1779, with no less forcible reason, denounced the like fatal consequences of these measures, and justly pointed out the alarming influence which the ill-timed and unfortunate enterprize from Bombay might have on the minds of the country powers, to the prejudice of the British interests; that they foresaw with justice that it might operate as an encouragement	The conduct of that presidency in regard to the Peshcush and the Guntoor Circar, seems, on the coolest and most deliberate examination of the reports, to have instigated the Nizam to the animation of a general confederacy of the country powers against the English. And we have more reason to form this judgment, as the Nizam, having once received satisfaction on those two articles, suffered this more than armed neutrality to come to nothing, at least

RESOLUTIONS. | OBSERVATIONS.

couragement to Hyder Ally "openly to resist the "proposed attempt on "Mahè;" that there was therein great foundation for their apprehensions of the unfavourable impression which those measures and events might fix in the disposition of the Nizam, already biassed against the company; that they represented with truth, the danger to which, in those circumstances, their northern Circars would be exposed, should the Nizam be induced to venture upon hostilities against them; that they therefore, with provident policy, resolved to send a resident to his Durbar, who might have the best intelligence of his temper and motions.

33. That the first ostensible design of the deputation to Hyderabad was perverted to a most impolitic and dishonourable purpose, by the steps taken for obtaining a relinquishment of the Peshcush, and as such tended rather to inflame

least as far as concerned himself. The *unjustifiable* proceedings against the Mahratta government were *justified* in three lines by the * Governor-general, and the Nizam acquiesced in the justification. Not but that the *real* causes of a war are seldom to be found in the manifestoes and public correspondence of the belligerant powers. The Nizam observed probably, that our armies had employment enough on their hands, and might conceive that to be the time to strike some beneficial stroke for himself—but he was mistaken.

---

* See his letter, 6th Report, p. 20. "We are "friends of the Peshwa and ministers, and shall con- "tinue so while they are our friends."

RESOLUTIONS.	OBSERVATIONS.
inflame than compose the resentment of the Nizam; which conduct was the more unpardonable in the president and select committee of Fort George, because they had apprehended, with such early and just foresight, the dangerous effects of his dissatisfaction and the necessity of averting it.	
34. That the motives as well as success of the Nizam's instigations, to form and animate a confederacy of the great country powers against the British possessions in India, and the calamitous events which ensued, may be properly attributed both to the unjustifiable proceedings against the Maratta government and to the conduct of the Madras presidency, in regard to the Peshcush and the Guntoor circar.	
35. That it appears, that the instructions and powers given to Colonel Goddard by the Superior Council on 5th April 1779, fixed on them from that time the chief direction and responsibility of the treaty and war with the Marattas.	Admitted on all hands.

The

Resolutions.	Observations.
36. That whatever backwardness was afterwards manifested by the Maratta ministers to any accommodation, unless upon very hard and humiliating terms to the company, must be ascribed as well to their too reasonable diffidence in our sincerity, as to their advantageous pretensions from the convention of Worgaum, and the well-known discontent or enmity which our conduct had raised in other powers against us.	The backwardness manifested by the Mahratta ministers to any accommodation, unless upon very hard and humiliating terms to the company, merely shews that they, like ourselves, wish to *make the most of the market*. But from the whole spirit of the Report, it is evident, that the *real* origin of all their backwardness was the advantage given them by our precipitate eagerness for peace on any terms at Poorunder.—From that moment they perceived the childish apprehensions which operated on the leading members of our government, and assumed extravagant pretensions and insolent language accordingly.
37. That it appears that the expences of the war, and especially of the detachment sent to the Malabar coast, were felt and acknowledged to be in a very serious degree distressing to the Bengal government, and greatly overbalanced every probable advantage from success, even before the irruption of Hyder Ally into the Carnatic	The immediate expences of every extensive war can only be re-imbursed by the long and gradual advantages of a good peace. It is certain, the charge of the detachment was very burthensome to Bengal—But that very burthen was a powerful spur to vigorous actions, and an additional plea for the acquisition, if

Resolutions.	Observations.
natic made the misfortune of being engaged at the same time in such a war with the Marattas more calamitous and alarming. 38. That immediately upon advice of the success of Hyder Ally in the Carnatic, the Governor-general and Council gave proof of the readiest and most important exertions for the assistance of the presidency of Madras, and took immediate measures with a view to obtain peace with the Marattas, and to regain the friendship of the Nizam. 39. That it must be reckoned among the many additional mischiefs which have arisen chiefly from this improvident war with the Marattas to the Company's affairs, that the military force of the Carnatic had been weakened by reinforcements sent to the Malabar coast; that the Bengal government have been under the necessity of supporting, on their confines, the army of a power confederated (however involuntarily) against them; that they have been obliged to sue for	if possible, of an adequate compensation. A dozen Machaons are worth an army: a good statesman is worth a dozen Machaons. In the midst of accumulated distress, and perplexed by the clamours of despair, Mr. Hastings planned and executed the relief of Madras. Rajah Chimnajee Boosla had stationed an army where he had a right to station it, in his own dominions; nor could our troops march to the Carnatic, without crossing those dominions: and the only possibility of saving the Carnatic depended on their passing unmolested. They did pass, and enabled Sir Eyre Coote to follow up his first doubtful victory over Hyder Ally, which was the origin of all our future success. Chimnajee, though not an enemy to our schemes, watched them with an interested solicitude; and having private political rules for his own conduct, would probably have profited by our ill-

RESOLUTIONS.	OBSERVATIONS.
for the mediation of the same power (the Raja of Berar) have submitted to a refusal, and purchased at last an uncertain, because apparently an unauthorized treaty on most extravagant and dishonourable conditions with his son Raja Chimnajee; and finally, that being burthened with the expences of a variety of distant expeditions while their allies are in distress and their tributaries under oppression, there is also an alarming deficiency in their own resources of revenue and commerce, by the accumulation of their debt and the reduction of their investment.	ill-success, as we could not, at that moment, guarantee him on a conjunction with us from the attempts of Nizam Ally—In this situation his alliance was of the utmost importance to us; and to those who know the perpetual arrears of payment due to Indian armies, it will not seem wonderful that the Raja should want money: To those who would vote a gratuitous donation of 26 lacks annually to the king, the purchase of part of Chimnajee's troops will seem very cheap at 16 lacks.
40. That	But it will be found impossible, by any number of Resolutions, to unravel all the intricate doublings of Asiatic policy. In countries where the balance of power is uncertain, contests are inevitable. New events give rise to new expedients, and those again to newer events. Ultimate success is the goal of each contending party. If we would obtain the end, we must not neglect the means. As the treaty with Raja Chimnajee was unau-

RESOLUTIONS.	OBSERVATIONS.
	unauthorized, the vigour of the measure is doubly honourable for the Governor-general. Instead of being extravagant, it has been proved *moderate*; and Mr. Hastings, with the most unexampled disinterestedness, staked his own private fortune to procure it.
40. That the attempt made by the Government General, in the month of January 1781, to form an engagement of alliance, offensive and defensive, with the Dutch East India Company, by the means, and upon the terms stated in the proceedings of their council, was unwarranted, impolitic, extravagant, and unjust.	The suddenness and success of the invasion by Hyder Ally, hardly left an option of measures for his repulse. State-necessity amply justified the offer of a small part of those territories, supposed to be captured by him, for the protection and recovery of the whole. Had the Carnatic been lost in the event of the invasion, and had Mr. Hastings never started the proposition of a possibility of Dutch assistance—the omission would have been branded with terms of equal condemnation, and with that justice which the present state of the case will not admit.
41. That it appears, that according to the last official dispatches from Bengal, dated 15 May 1781, the prospect of peace	Overturned (while pending) by an undoubted and favourable change of affairs. The

Resolutions.	Observations.
peace was not then propitious, because it did not seem to be wished for by the Marattas upon the terms proposed, and because the government of Bengal not thinking it desirable, without obtaining even additional advantages, had reprobated the system of defence, which the Presidency of Bombay wished to have adopted; and that the conduct of the Government General, as far as it might tend to procrastinate accommodation with the Marattas, was evidently injurious to the interests of the Company and to the Nation.	
42. That it appears, that the Government General had been previously in possession of a letter from the Duan of the Rajah of Berar, containing overtures for mediation for peace, and alliance with the Peshwa; and that this material information was wholly suppressed by them in their dispatches to the Court of Directors, but a copy of it was sent by the same conveyance to the private Agent of Mr. Hastings;	The Government General might as well be deemed responsible for the arrival of all the Company's ships at a precise date, or the continuance of the monsoon a month beyond the periodical change. The failure of the intelligence in question depended on events out of the reach of human foresight or precaution. Mr. Hastings's private Agent is alone accountable, and has already accounted for the

RESOLUTIONS.	OBSERVATIONS.

Hastings; and that in thus neglecting to make immediate communication to the Court of Directors of such important intelligence, the Government General appear to have failed in an essential part of their duty.

43. That it appears, that the Court of Directors, in their latest dispatches, have given instructions, which, if duly obeyed by their governments in India, may have already perfected the desirable work of peace; and that every encouragement and assistance which may be thought necessary, should be given by parliament to expedite the accomplishment of it: "That the principle of "pacification may be ex-"tended as soon as possi-"ble to a general restora-"tion of tranquillity with "all the neighbouring "powers, on terms of the "most perfect modera-"tion, in order that the "honour of the nation "may be retrieved, and "the several governments "may be able to lessen "their own insupportable "charges,

the circumstance with full satisfaction.

The *due* obedience to be given in India to orders issued from Europe, must depend on the state of affairs when those orders shall arrive. If parliament shall think fit to annul the existence of all discretionary powers, as held by the Company's confidential servants, those servants will of course implicitly submit—But if otherwise, the conduct of the Governor-general through all his administration, and as displayed in the several pages of the Reports, leaves no room to doubt of his readiness, of his desire, and of his ability, to procure a proper completion to every paragraph of the Company's late orders.

The

Resolutions.	Observations.

"charges, and to relieve their friends and allies from additional expences and oppressions incurred on account of war; and also that they may be able to exert their whole force against the national enemies, if the continuance of European troubles should make it necessary."

44. That for the purpose of conveying entire conviction to the minds of the native princes, that to commence hostilities without just provocation against them, and to pursue schemes of conquest and extent of dominion, are measures repugnant to the wish, the honour, and the policy of this nation; the parliament of Great Britain should give some signal mark of its displeasure against those, in whatever degree entrusted with the charge of the East India Company's affairs, who shall appear to have wilfully adopted or countenanced a system tending to inspire a reasonable distrust of the moderation, justice, and good faith of the British nation.

The wisdom of parliament will, no doubt, co-operate with its justice in the selection of the proper objects of its displeasure. As the blow will be severely felt, its direction will be maturely weighed. From the strict impartiality, the unerring judgement, and exemplary moderation of the British legislature, he would be unworthy the name of a Briton, who could feel a wish, or drop a hint, to remove his cause.

www.ingramcontent.com/pod-product-compliance
Lightning Source LLC
Chambersburg PA
CBHW031551110426
42739CB00039B/1084